Food *for* Hope

First published in 2013
by Londubh Books, 18 Casimir Avenue, Harold's Cross, Dublin 6w
www.londubh.ie
and the Irish Motor Neurone Disease Association,
Coleraine House, Coleraine Street, Dublin 7
www.imnda.ie
1 3 5 4 2

Origination by David Parfrey; cover by bluett

Printed by Gráficas Castuera, Navarra, Spain

ISBN: 978-1-907535-31-4

Food for Hope

A Cookbook in Support of
the Irish Motor Neurone Disease Association

Edited by Katie Hallissey

Contents

Spaghetti all'Arrabbiata 47
Chris de Burgh

Paula Meehan's Jade Soup 49
Theo Dorgan

Chinese Braised Beef 50
Joe Duffy

Monday Curry 53
John Duhan

Strawberry Tiramisu 54
Eileen Dunne

CocoChocNut Cookies 55
Bernard Farrell

Beef Stir Fry 59
Catherine Fulvio

Mushroom Soup 61
Pat Gilroy

Salmon Quiche 62
Orla Hardiman

French Toast with a Twist 65
Dermot Healy

Roast Beef with Stuffing 66
Hermitage Green

Tom's New York Pasta 68
Tom Hickey

Treacle and Ginger Bread 70
President Michael D. and Sabina Higgins

Chicken and Broccoli Bake 71
Amy Huberman

T-Bone Steak and Sides 72
Tom Jordan

Stir Fried Pork Fillet 75
Enda Kenny

Piccata Milanese 77
Bobby Kerr

Strawberry Mascarpone Cake 79
Laura Kilkenny

Traditional Colcannon 81
John Lonergan

Tom Yum Soup 82
Jack Lukeman

Iveragh Harvest Chowder 84
Kathleen Lynch

Wedding Cake 87
John MacKenna

Irish Stew 88
Jimmy Magee

Introduction

Thank you for purchasing *Food for Hope*, a book of recipes donated by your favourite Irish celebrities and enlivened by their accompanying anecdotes. We hope you enjoy the book and the mouthwatering photographs that complement the content throughout and that you sample some of the recipes.

Many wonderful people have contributed to *Food for Hope*, all sharing the goal of supporting the Irish Motor Neurone Disease Association, which for the past twenty-eight years has been the primary support organisation in Ireland for people with motor neurone disease (MND), their families and carers.

As well as practical help, such as a dedicated MND nurse, financial assistance towards home care and specialist medical assistance, the IMNDA provides advice and support to empower those with MND in their lives. With patients as its focus, the association does all it can to enable anybody living with MND to receive the best care, achieve the highest possible quality of life and die with dignity.

My family and I experienced at first hand the impressive work of the association in terms of practical support and counselling. During the arduous battle my father John fought with the disease, the IMNDA helped him to keep his face towards the sunshine at times when he felt trapped in a body that knew only rain. His charitable nature and his appreciation of all the IMNDA did for him live on in me.

Thinking about how to bring MND to the forefront of the public mind and provide a platform for people of all walks of life who have been touched by this disease to unite in support, I began to recall moments I shared with my father across the kitchen table. I thought about how mealtimes can act as a glue in any family, a time to come together, a time to laugh, or even to cry. With all this in mind, the *Food for Hope* project was born.

As with any project, it has taken 'many hands to make light work'. It has been a truly fulfilling experience bringing this book together with a team of such wonderful people. My good friend, Marie Reavey, dedicated regional fundraiser with the IMNDA, and I had the pleasure of meeting Dolores MacKenna, whose family's contribution to this book has been pivotal. For this we are so grateful. Having experienced MND in their families, Marie and Dolores have an understanding of the disease and an enthusiasm for this project that have been an enormous help to me.

One of the most poignant moments in the creation of *Food for Hope* occurred in relation to the late Maeve Binchy. Dolores, an old acquaintance of Maeve, wrote to her and her husband Gordon Snell to ask for their support for the book. This letter from Dolores, published in *The Irish Times* on 3 August 2012, speaks for itself:

Sir: On Tuesday morning last I woke to the sad news of Maeve Binchy's death. Downstairs I found a letter from Gordon, Maeve's husband, enclosing a recipe, at Maeve's request, as a contribution to a book of recipes I am helping to compile to raise funds for the Irish Motor Neurone Disease Association. One of the last kind gestures of a wonderfully generous woman.

We are especially grateful to the well known Irish people from all walks of life who generously contributed recipes. We would also like to thank our talented photographers: Michael O'Meara of Oscar's Restaurant, Galway, Fergal O'Callaghan and Alan Butler; also Jess Walsh, Galway, whose family was recently affected by MND.

Thank you to our sponsors for their financial support for the project.

Finally, a warm thank you to our publisher, Jo O'Donoghue of Londubh Books. Jo is herself familiar with MND, having lost her father to the disease, and her devotion to the cause never faltered throughout these past months.

Currently there are approximately three hundred patients in Ireland living with MND and registered with the association. We are optimistic that *Food for Hope* will raise awareness of this disease as well as much-needed funds for the IMNDA.

You will find the recipes in this cookbook in alphabetical order by the name of the contributor. May you enjoy the *Food for Hope* experience as much as we enjoyed bringing it to you.

Katie Hallissey, May 2013

Cauliflower and Broccoli Soup
Gerry Adams TD

This tasty soup serves 6-8.

1 litre chicken or vegetable stock
1 head cauliflower
3 heads broccoli
2 onions

200g Parmesan, grated
freshly ground black pepper
85ml (⅓ of 250ml tub)
double cream

1   Chop up the onions and vegetables and add to the stock. Add half the Parmesan and the black pepper and simmer for twenty minutes.

2   Add the rest of the Parmesan and the cream, put into a blender and pulse until smooth. Return to the saucepan and simmer for five to ten minutes.

Warm Salad of Fillet of Irish Beef with Mustard and Horseradish Mayonnaise and French Fried Onions

Darina Allen, Food Writer and Teacher

The mere mention of French fried onions puts fear and dread into those watching their figures but these involve only a little milk and seasoned flour so they have a delicious crisp coating. Recently, my nephew Ivan Whelan gave me a great tip: he found that when he added a lightly whisked egg white to the milk it made the onion rings even crispier.

The watch point here is not to cut the onion rings more thickly than the recipe calls for, or else the coating will be overcooked while the onions are still raw. French fried onions are wonderful with beef, but we pile them up on salads and pan-fried venison, too. Paprika, Sichuan pepper, cumin or coriander can be added to the flour to ring the changes.

Mustard and Horseradish Mayonnaise

2 egg yolks
2 tbsp Dijon mustard
1 tbsp sugar
2 tbsp wine vinegar
150ml olive oil or sunflower oil
1 tbsp grated fresh horseradish
1 tsp chopped parsley

French Fried Onions

1 egg white
300ml milk
2 large onions, peeled
225g seasoned flour
good-quality oil or beef dripping
    for deep frying

1 thin slice of fillet of Irish beef
    per person
selection of salad leaves

Tarragon Dressing

4 tbsp olive oil
4 tbsp sunflower oil
2 tbsp white wine vinegar
pinch mustard
salt, freshly ground pepper and
    pinch sugar
1 tbsp chopped tarragon

1   Put the egg yolks into a bowl. Add the mustard, sugar, wine vinegar and mix well. Whisk in the oil very gradually. Finally, add the grated horseradish and chopped parsley. Taste and season if necessary.

2   Whisk the egg white lightly and add to the milk.

3   Slice the onion into 5mm rings around the middle. Separate the rings and cover with the milk mixture until needed. (The leftover milk may be boiled up, thickened with roux and used for a white or parsley sauce).

4   Just before serving, heat the oil or beef dripping to 180°C. Toss the rings a few at a time in well-seasoned flour. Deep-fry in the hot oil for 2-3 minutes or until golden.

5   Drain on kitchen paper and serve hot.

6   Heat a small frying pan with a little olive oil or butter. Put the slices of beef on the pan and season with salt and pepper.

7   While the beef is cooking, make the tarragon dressing by mixing the ingredients together Toss the salad leaves in just enough of the dressing to coat the leaves.

8   Divide the leaves between four warm plates or put on one large serving dish. Place the cooked slices of beef on top of the salad. Spoon a little of the horseradish mayonnaise on each slice of beef and pile onion rings on top. Serve immediately.

Beef in Guinness
Aslan, Rock Band

2 large onions, chopped
1 garlic clove, crushed
olive oil for frying
1kg rib steak, cut into chunks
6 tbsp plain flour, well seasoned
   with salt and freshly
   ground pepper

500ml can Guinness
beef stock, fresh, cube or
   concentrate made up to 250ml
   (or water)
sprig thyme and bay leaf tied
   together
parsley or other herbs to garnish

1   In a large casserole, fry the chopped onion gently in a little olive oil until softened and translucent. Add the garlic and fry briefly, making sure not to brown. Remove the onion and garlic from the pan and put aside on a plate.

2   Add a little extra olive oil, dust the braising steak with seasoned flour (a plastic bag is good for this) and brown in the hot pan, turning to make sure that all surfaces are browned.

3   When the beef has a good, even colour, scrape off any flour that has stuck to the bottom of the casserole and put the onions and garlic back with the meat. Pour in the Guinness and top up with the stock or water to cover the beef. Add the thyme and bay leaf.

4   Cover the casserole and cook in the middle of the oven, 150°C/gas 3, for 2-3 hours until the beef is meltingly tender. Check after 2 hours, add a little more liquid if necessary and remove the herbs.

5   Before serving, check seasoning and garnish with chopped parsley or other herbs.

6   Serve with boiled or mashed potatoes or plain boiled rice. For a special occasion serve with colcannon.

Potato Cakes and Mackerel Smokies
Maeve Binchy and Gordon Snell, Writers

*These recipes in verse are from the pen of Gordon Snell, published in
a collection called* The Rhyming Irish Cookbook *(1992).*

Potato Cakes
1kg mashed potatoes
110g plain or self-raising flour
25g butter, melted
70ml milk
Salt to season

Mackerel Smokies
500g smoked mackerel
8 ramekins or pots and butter
   to grease them
12 button mushrooms
250ml cream
grated Parmesan
freshly ground black pepper
   to season

(Preheat the oven to 190°C/gas 5.)

1 Flour, milk salt and butter
    That's all it really takes,
    With cooked and mashed potato,
    To make potato cakes.

2 Mix them all together
    And then roll out the dough;
    Cut it into rounds or squares
    A half-inch thick or so.

3 Fry them for three minutes
    In a heavy bottomed pan,
    Then turn and fry the other side –
    Resist them if you can!

4 This is easy – all it takes
    Is breaking mackerel into flakes;
    Then just rub some butter in
    To each pot or ramekin.

5 Nearly fill each little dish
    With a portion of the fish
    Add the mushrooms, sliced quite thin;
    The pepper and the cream put in,

6 And sprinkle on some Parmesan.
    It's time the cooking now began.
    Twenty minutes will complete, at a
      moderate heat.
    The reaction you'll provoke is:
      'Wow! I love these
      mackerel smokies!'

Vegetable Curry
Frances Black, Singer

I was delighted to be asked to support IMNDA by providing a recipe for this book. Motor neurone disease is a devastating illness for the individual and their family, and the work that IMNDA do is fantastic. This is a lovely comforting dish to have on a cold winter's evening. I like to serve it with garlic naan bread.

Curry base sauce
100g red lentils
2 medium onions, peeled and
    roughly chopped
3 medium carrots, roughly
    chopped
1 red pepper, deseeded and
    roughly chopped
1 tbsp light olive oil or vegetable
    oil
6 cloves garlic, peeled and
    roughly chopped
70g fresh ginger, peeled and
    roughly chopped
6 stalks coriander, chopped
1 whole red chilli, deseeded and
    roughly chopped
1 tbsp each ground coriander,
    cumin, cinnamon, paprika,
    turmeric and garam masala
½ tsp ground black pepper
2 x 400 g can plum tomatoes
300ml water
200ml can coconut milk
Salt to taste

Curried vegetables
1 tbsp vegetable oil
1 medium red onion, peeled and
    chopped
1 courgette, diced
2 carrots, diced
½ butternut squash, peeled and
    diced
100g mushrooms, quartered
1 red pepper, diced
150g cauliflower, broken into florets
50g chickpeas, cooked
600ml curry base sauce
400ml water

1   Wash the lentils, place them in a pan and cover with cold water. Bring to the boil and simmer gently for 15-20 minutes, until tender. Meanwhile, blitz all the vegetables, garlic and ginger in a food processor. Heat enough oil to cover the bottom of a large saucepan, add the spices and fry gently for a couple of minutes. Then add the onions, carrots, pepper, garlic, ginger, coriander stalks, the chilli and all the spices and fry over a low heat for 5-10 minutes until the onions start to soften.

2   Add the tomatoes, water and lentils and simmer for another 30 minutes before adding the coconut milk. Bring to the boil, then remove from the heat and blend until smooth, using a hand blender. Season to taste. Set aside to cool, then use as required.

3   Fry the onion gently for 10 minutes in a little vegetable oil in a large pan, then add the remaining vegetables and chickpeas and stir. Add the curry base sauce and simmer gently for 25-30 minutes, taking care not to overcook the vegetables. If the sauce becomes too thick, add a little water to give the desired consistency.

Herb Crust Rack of Lamb

Derek Blount, the Wicklow Heather Restaurant, Laragh, County Wicklow

*I am delighted to pass on this recipe to support this worthy cause.
You can ask your butcher to 'French trim' your rack of lamb,
removing all the fat.*

Herb Crust
200g parsley
100g basil
100g mint
2 cloves garlic
300g dried breadcrumbs
50ml olive oil

2x8-bone rack of lamb
    (French trimmed)
50g honey
50g English mustard
salt and pepper

1   Remove all the large stalks from the herbs and place in a food processor with garlic and breadcrumbs. Blitz for 3-5 minutes. Add oil and continue to blitz for a further 30 seconds. Leave at room temperature until ready to use.

2   Season the lamb with salt and pepper and seal in a frying pan over a high heat (approximately 2-3 minutes each side).

3   Place in a pre-heated roasting dish oven at 180°C/gas 4 and roast according to taste, 15-18 minutes for medium, about 25 minutes for well done. Approximately 3 minutes before cooking is complete, remove from the oven. Mix the honey and mustard and brush the lamb with it. Dip the coated lamb into the herb crust mixture and return to the oven for 3-4 minutes.

Fish and Chips with Gram Flour Batter and Tartare Sauce

Maclean Burke, Actor

The most important thing is that the fish should be fresh. Sunflower oil is my favourite for a crisp, light batter. Using gram (chick pea) flour as a substitute for wheat flour makes a lovely coating on the fish and is simple to prepare. The potatoes I prefer for making chips are Maris Pipers.

Batter

300ml chilled water
2 eggs
300g gram flour
1 clove garlic, finely chopped
30g chopped parsley
salt and pepper to season

Tartare Sauce

1 hardboiled egg
100ml mayonnaise
juice of ½ lemon
1 tsp each chopped capers,
    gherkins and parsley

1   Beat or blend all the ingredients for the batter together until smooth.

2   Dredge the fish in a little flour, then dip in the batter. Shake off any excess batter and carefully fry the fish in clean oil that has been heated to 180°C. Cook until golden on all sides. You know the fish is cooked when the flesh separates into flakes.

3   For the tartare sauce mash the egg and mayonnaise and add the other ingredients. Mix well.

4   Peel the potatoes and slice into chips, then leave to soak for a few hours in cold water. Drain and dry thoroughly, then fry in oil at 120°C until cooked but without colour.

5   Remove from the oil and raise the temperature to 180°C, then fry the chips in the hot oil until golden. To serve, toss in a little Japanese rice wine vinegar and sea salt.

Chicken Tagine with Apricots
Gabriel Byrne, Actor

This delicious dish takes just ten minutes to prepare and forty minutes to cook.

3 tbsp olive oil
8 small chicken thighs
   (2 per person)
salt and freshly ground pepper
   for seasoning
2 medium onions, chopped
2 garlic cloves, chopped
large pinch saffron threads,
   crushed
1 tsp ground ginger

1 tsp ground cumin
1 tsp ground cinnamon
10 ready-to-eat dried apricots,
   cut into quarters
juice of 1 lemon
2 tbsp honey
small handful chopped coriander
300ml chicken stock (or water)
4 tbsp flaked almonds, toasted,
   for garnish

1   In a large, heavy saucepan, heat a little of the olive oil. Season the chicken thighs and brown on both sides. Remove from the pan and set aside. Add to the pan the remaining oil, onions, garlic and some salt and pepper. Sauté gently for 20 minutes until softened and golden.

2   Add the spices, sauté for 1 minute, then add the chickens, apricots, lemon juice, honey and half the coriander. Pour in the stock or water and cook on a low heat for 30 minutes, or until the chicken is tender. Sprinkle with the almonds and remaining coriander and serve with warm couscous.

Roast Rabbit à la Ballyderrig

Gay Byrne, Broadcaster

This was a favourite recipe of my mother. I hope you like it.

1 rabbit
300ml vinegar
600ml water
50g butter
1 tbsp flour, seasoned

pinch pepper
4 rashers of bacon, chopped
1 tbsp parsley, chopped
2 onions, diced
300ml hot milk

1   Cut the rabbit into pieces after soaking it in vinegar and water.

2   Coat the pieces in the seasoned flour and brown them in butter.

3   Place in a casserole, adding the chopped bacon, parsley, onions and hot milk.

4   Cover and bake for one hour in a moderate oven, 180ºC/gas 4.

Chocolate Chews
Damian Clarke, Comedian

I can't cook but I make desserts.
Here is the recipe for chocolate chews, no oven required!

6 tsp cocoa
300g sugar (use a tad less if your
    dentist is an angry man)
100ml milk
50g butter or other shortening
    (I used Copha in Australia)

350g rolled oats
dash of vanilla essence
50g desiccated coconut
pinch of salt (optional)
whatever else you wish,
    for the laugh

1   Dump the cocoa, sugar, milk and butter into a pot and bring to the boil.

2   Add the dry ingredients.

3   Drop the mixture on to waxed paper in biscuit-size lumps, or use paper cupcake holders. Makes about 36, enough for a meal for one in front of the telly.

4   Let the mixture cool, then chuck the tray in the fridge for 40-60 minutes until the chews go hard.

5   Bon appétit.

Bunbelievables with Chocolate Ganache
Catherine Cleary, Journalist

These are cup cakes that substitute agave syrup for sugar and still taste yummy, thanks to the quality of the ingredients. The recipe makes between twenty and twenty-four cup cakes, depending on the size of your cases.

Bunbelievables

400g plain flour
2 tsp baking soda
1½ tsp salt
60g pure cacao, finely grated
8 tsp sugar-free cocoa powder
120g butter (melted)
120ml grapeseed oil
320ml agave syrup
320ml milk
2 tsp white wine vinegar

Chocolate Ganache

120ml heavy cream
120ml maple syrup
100g Willie's Supreme Raw Cacao
   (Blue Venezuelan)
180g butter
50g hazelnuts toasted, skinned
   and chopped finely

1   Heat the oven to 180°C. In order put all the ingredients into a food processor and mix to a lump-free batter. Line the bun tins with paper cases. Fill each one three quarters full with batter. Bake for 20-25 five minutes until firm. Cool on a wire tray.

2   Heat the cream and maple syrup in a pan. Bring to the boil, whisking it gently.

3   Turn off the heat and add the chopped cacao, stirring until melted.

4   Stir in the butter one tablespoon at a time, waiting until each one is melted before adding the next.

5   Transfer the mixture to a bowl and cool in the fridge until it has thickened to a piping consistency.

6   Top the buns with the cooled ganache, using a palette knife or an icing bag to pipe it in a circular design. Finish with a sprinkle of chopped toasted hazelnuts.

Prawn Linguine with a Kick
Simon Coveney TD,
Minister for Agriculture, Food and the Marine

I never have much time at home so anything I cook needs to be fairly fast to prepare. Cork is a great place for seafood, with fresh fish readily available. I'm honoured to be associated with the Irish Motor Neurone Disease Association and wish them well in all the very important work they are doing.

about 24 fresh tiger prawns
50g unsalted butter
2-3 garlic cloves, crushed
12 spring onions, thinly sliced

1 red chilli pepper, deseeded
    and finely chopped
4 tbsp white wine
400ml cream
500g linguine

1   Peel, top, tail and de-vein the prawns.

2   In a non-stick pan gently melt the butter. Add the crushed garlic and half the spring onions and the chopped chilli and cook over a low heat for a minute or so.

3   Add the prawns and cook for around 6 minutes until they turn pink. Add a tablespoon or two of white wine and heat for a minute, then add the cream (up to 400ml) and simmer gently for four or five minutes.

4   Cook the linguine in boiling water for 8 to 10 minutes until *al dente*. Drain and add to the pan containing the prawns and heat everything through. Add the remaining spring onions and season with salt and pepper to taste.

5   Toss and serve with fresh crusty bread.

Chicken and Vegetable Curry
Una Crawford, Actor

2 tbsp oil

1 onion, roughly chopped

2 cloves garlic, crushed

1 tsp ground cumin

1 tsp ground coriander

1 tsp turmeric

2-3 tsp chilli flakes

4 chicken fillets, cubed

2 potatoes, cubed

2 carrots, cut into batons

6 baby sweetcorn

half a cauliflower, cut into
   small florets

450ml chicken or vegetable stock

2 tbsp tomato purée

pinch salt and pepper

1 tsp garam masala

2 heaped tbsp crème fraîche

1   Heat the oil in a frying pan with a heavy base. Fry the onion and garlic gently until slightly softened. Add the cumin, coriander, turmeric and chilli and fry for a couple of minutes. Add the chicken and cook for about 3 minutes.

2   Add the potatoes, carrots, baby sweetcorn and cauliflower. Add the stock and tomato purée and season with salt and pepper.

3   Cover and leave to simmer for 45 minutes to an hour. Stir in the garam masala and the crème fraîche. Serve with lots of rice, poppadoms and naan bread.

Meatballs with Tomato Sauce and Roasted Tomato Garnish

John Crown, Oncologist and Senator

Meatballs

1 kg organic minced beef
1 medium onion finely chopped
    and lightly fried in a little
    olive oil
50g breadcrumbs
50g Parmesan, finely grated
dash Worcester sauce
50ml tomato ketchup
small handful fresh parsley, finely
    chopped

Tomato Sauce

1 medium onion, finely chopped
2 cloves garlic, crushed
10ml olive oil
1 tin chopped tomatoes
20ml tomato purée
50g roast red peppers
1 small red chilli, deseeded and
    finely chopped
1 tsp sugar
50g fresh basil

1 For the meatballs, mix all the ingredients together. Form into 20 balls about the size of golf balls.

2 For the tomato sauce, sweat the onion and garlic in olive oil in a heavy pot until the onions are soft but not coloured. Add the tomatoes, tomato purée, roast peppers, chilli and sugar and allow to simmer for about an hour. Season with salt and freshly ground black pepper. Add the basil at the end of the cooking time so that it keeps its colour.

3 Seal the meatballs in a hot frying pan, then place into a deep roasting dish. Cover with the tomato sauce and cook in the oven at 180°C/gas 4 for 35-40 minutes.

4 For the tomato garnish, toss 20 cherry tomatoes in 2 tablespoons olive oil with 5 cloves garlic and a bay leaf. Season with salt and freshly ground black pepper. Place on a tray and roast at 140°C/gas 4 for about an hour, then at 80°C/gas 1 for a further hour.

5 To serve simply cook pasta of your choice, spoon the meatballs on top of the pasta, add plenty of tomato sauce and garnish with the roasted cherry tomatoes.

Risotto with Mushrooms, Peas and Spinach
Leo Cullen, Rugby Player

10-15g dried porcini mushrooms
olive oil
1 clove garlic, finely minced
1 tbsp chopped parsley
30g butter
2 tbsp finely chopped onion
250g flavourful mushrooms
    cleaned and cut into halves

1 litre chicken stock
300g arborio rice
125ml white wine
70g frozen peas
100g spinach, chopped
5 tbsp grated Parmesan

1   Place the porcini mushrooms in a small bowl with 250ml boiling water and allow to sit for thirty minutes. Strain the liquid into a saucepan with the stock. This should be brought to a gentle simmer, to be added at intervals to the rice.

2   Heat the olive oil in a frying pan, add the garlic and the porcini and cook for about two minutes. Add the chopped parsley, stir and remove from the heat.

3   Melt the butter in a saucepan, add the onion and mushrooms and sauté for five minutes. Add the rice and stir to combine. Add the wine and stir until it is completely absorbed. Proceed to add the stock, one ladle at a time, and continue to stir. When it has been absorbed you can add the next amount and so on.

4   After ten minutes, add the peas and the porcini. A few minutes later add the spinach.

5   The total cooking time should be about twenty minutes. The rice should be tender but still firm. Finally add the Parmesan and a little extra stock. If you are feeling bold you could add some cream. The consistency of the risotto is very important. The rice should be loose and creamy, so add more stock if necessary.

6   When serving, you could drizzle a small drop of truffle olive oil over each portion. Enjoy!

Chocolate Brandy Cake
Catherine Cusack, Actor

I have to confess that I am no cook so I have shamelessly stolen an old friend's recipe. I could have chosen the horror of boiled tripe, one of my father Cyril Cusack's favourites, but I thought I'd spare you. My father could also have a sweet tooth and he wouldn't have minded the brandy. Actually he would probably have asked for a whiskey substitution.

All I would like to say is that coping with and watching someone go through MND was the severest test of my life. I have the greatest admiration and sympathy for anyone who is dealing with this condition, patient or carer.

200g dark chocolate
200g butter
200g digestive biscuits
2 eggs
85g sugar

50g glacé cherries
50g ground walnuts
small glass of brandy (optional but I would say mandatory)
strips of angelica to decorate

1　Melt the chocolate and the butter together over a very low heat.

2　In a plastic bag crush the biscuits coarsely with a rolling pin.

3　Beat the eggs and sugar together until creamy, then stir into the melted chocolate and butter.

4　Add most of the cherries and walnuts, crushed biscuits and brandy.

5　Put in a buttered mould or a 'push up' cake tin. Decorate with the remaining cherries, walnuts and strips of angelica and leave in the fridge to chill.

6　To serve, cut into thin slices and serve with fresh strawberries or raspberries and whipped cream.

Everyday Risotto
Niamh Cusack, Actor

This is what everyone in our house regards as a staple – a 'there's nothing in the fridge; what'll we have without going to the supermarket' kind of dish. I never tire of it, which may of course mean I'm a bit dull.

But my mother, who was not dull, made something similar when I was growing up in the 1960s and 1970s. She didn't have risotto rice so she made it with basmati and we thought it was a real treat! My father Cyril was a stranger to the kitchen, so the only link between him and this recipe is that he was occasionally lucky enough not to be out at the theatre when she made it!

1 tbsp olive oil for frying
1 large red onion, finely chopped
2 cloves garlic, finely chopped
½ fresh red chilli, finely chopped
½ head celery, finely chopped

400g risotto rice
400g tin chopped tomatoes
1 litre chicken or vegetable stock
2 handfuls frozen peas
100g Parmesan

1   Heat the olive oil in a deep frying pan or large saucepan. Fry the onion, garlic and chilli over a gentle flame, stirring all the time, for about 5 minutes. Add the celery and sauté for 5 minutes, stirring continuously. Add the rice and fry for about 3 minutes till it becomes translucent. Keep stirring.

2   Add the chopped tomatoes, stirring until they're absorbed. Bit by bit, while stirring continuously for about 15 minutes, add the stock until it has all been absorbed into the rice. Add the peas with the last 300ml of stock, stirring gently.

3   When all the liquid has been absorbed, add the Parmesan and leave to stand for 2 minutes.

4   Serve with a green salad.

Cheese Soufflé
Pádraig Cusack, Theatre Producer

My mum was a great cook and one of those people who could create something out of apparently nothing. Those Friday evenings, when the fridge had little more than a bit of mouldy old cheddar, half a pint of milk and a knob or two of butter, the magic of cheese soufflé happened, aided by the fact that we had potatoes, lettuces and cucumbers in the garden. Magically, within an hour, there was what my sister Niamh and I thought the best dinner in the world.

30g butter plus a little extra for buttering the soufflé dish
25g plain flour
50ml milk
1 tsp grated nutmeg

Pinch sea salt and freshly ground black pepper
½ tsp Dijon mustard
4 eggs
100g grated mature red cheddar or any hard cheese
20g finely grated Parmesan

1   Pre-heat the oven to 190°C/gas 5. Butter generously the base and sides of an 800ml soufflé dish.

2   In a medium size heavy-bottomed saucepan, melt the butter. Add the flour and stir over a medium heat for about 2 minutes. Gradually add the milk, stirring constantly. Allow to simmer for another couple of minutes, stirring occasionally. Add the mustard, nutmeg and a good pinch of salt and pepper, stir once again, then set aside to cool a little.

3   Separate the eggs and put the whites in a bowl big enough for whisking but don't whisk them yet. Beat the yolks in a small bowl and set aside.

4   Return to the sauce and add the cheddar and most of the Parmesan, stirring it until it starts to blend. The sauce sometimes can look a little gloopy and bumpy at this stage but don't worry – it will be fine! Next, add the beaten yolks to the sauce and stir in fully. Remove from the heat.

5   Now, the next bit makes all the difference to any soufflé – the egg whites. You need to whisk them until they are stiff but if you over-whisk them they collapse so the secret is in knowing when to stop. Never whisk them in advance as even in the space of 5 minutes, they'll flop and so will your soufflé!! Whisk at a moderate speed until they start to peak. When you lift your whisk out of the whites and you are left with peaks, they're ready.

6   Take two tablespoons of egg white and mix it into the sauce to loosen it up. With a metal spoon, add the remainder of the egg whites to the sauce, folding them in carefully to keep it as airy as possible.

7   Pour the mix into your pre-buttered soufflé dish, sprinkle the remaining Parmesan on the top and place on a baking sheet in the centre of your oven. After about 35 minutes it should have risen nicely to impress your family or guests! Make sure everyone is sitting at the table and ready to eat so that they see the soufflé when you take it out of the oven. We always had soufflé with baked potatoes and a big green salad.

Summer Tart
Ita Daly, Writer

The idea for this delicious tart came to me one evening when I discovered that I had rhubarb and strawberries but not enough of either to fill a tart. I took a chance and combined both and it is truly a marriage made in heaven. The two flavours just complement one another perfectly. Also our strawberries often disappoint as we don't get enough sun, so cooking them very lightly in this manner overcomes this problem.

175g shortcrust pastry
(shop-bought is fine)
250g rhubarb

50g sugar
6 or 7 large strawberries

1   Roll out pastry to fit an 8-inch flat tin and bake this blind in the oven for about 15 minutes at 190°C/gas 5. The pastry should have a nice golden colour when you take it out. Leave it to cool when you get on with the filling.

2   Cut the rhubarb into short pieces and put it in a saucepan on a low heat to cook with a small quantity of water. Let the pieces soften but they should retain their shape. Add sugar and stir. Add the strawberries, cut in half, and leave to soften for about 2 minutes. Take off the heat and leave to cool.

3   Poor the filling into the pastry case, smoothing the top. Boil some sugar to a light, golden caramel and very carefully and slowly pour it over the tart in thin streams, forming any pattern that pleases you. Store in a cool place (not a fridge) and eat within 12 hours.

Spaghetti all'Arrabbiata

Chris de Burgh, Singer

This dish is terrific to have after one of the many concerts I do every year all over the world: Italian restaurants are often the only ones open late at night!! It is also easy to make at home. Make sure you add enough chilli to give it that extra 'zing' required for the dish to taste really great.

1 tbsp olive oil
1 garlic clove, chopped
1 tsp dried chilli flakes or
   peperoncino
1 tsp red wine vinegar
1 tbsp chopped fresh thyme
   (optional)

a few fried sage leaves (optional)
200g can cherry tomatoes
250g spaghetti, cooked according
   to instructions on packet
fresh chives, chopped, to serve
sea salt and freshly ground
   black pepper

1   Heat the oil in a deep frying pan, add the garlic and chilli flakes and cook over a low heat for three minutes. Also add the red wine vinegar, fresh thyme and sage leaves if you wish to use them.

2   Add the cherry tomatoes and cook for 4-5 minutes, until the tomatoes are beginning to break down.

3   Stir the sauce through the cooked spaghetti.

4   To serve, place in a bowl. Garnish with chives and season with salt and pepper.

Paula Meehan's Jade Soup

Theo Dorgan, Writer

Why 'jade' soup? The colour.

2 medium onions
1 whole bulb garlic
1 stick celery
1 tbsp olive oil
1-2 heaped tsp ground cumin
2 litres stock (fresh chicken stock or
    organic vegetable bouillon)

small handful fresh lovage
    or fresh coriander, chopped
1 bag (250g) organic spinach,
    washed
1 can coconut milk
sea salt and freshly ground black
    pepper to taste

1   Roughly chop the onions, garlic and celery and soften in the olive oil with the cumin. Add the stock with the lovage or coriander, bring to the boil and quickly lower to a steady simmer.

2   Add the spinach and when it has softened blend the soup (it's easiest to use an electric wand). Then add the coconut milk and whisk. Allow to simmer gently for a few minutes. Add salt and pepper to taste before serving.

3   For a thicker soup add a large boiled potato, chopped, before blending.

4   For a spicier soup add 1 or 2 seeded and chopped jalapeño peppers to the onion and garlic for softening.

5   Serve with a dollop of plain set yogurt or crème fraîche in each bowl.

Chinese Braised Beef

Joe Duffy, Broadcaster

I think this is a simple and lovely way to cook meat. Star anise, now widely available in Ireland, along with the soy sauce and garlic, gives it a most distinctive taste. Unlike most Chinese recipes, this can be left quietly cooking on top of the stove. Eat with roasted Rooster potatoes and my favourite vegetables, Brussels sprouts tossed in Dalkey mustard, and you can't go wrong.

2 tbsp vegetable oil
1kg topside of beef, tied
2 tbsp dark soy sauce
2 tbsp dry sherry
2 cloves garlic, peeled

1 star anise flower
1 tbsp sugar
freshly ground black pepper
radish roses
spring onion

1 Heat the oil in a small deep flameproof casserole, add the beef and fry over a brisk heat, turning often, to brown on all sides.

2 Add the soy sauce, sherry and garlic and bring to the boil. Add anise, cover and cook over a very gentle heat for an hour or until cooked through.

3 Turn the beef, add the sugar, sprinkle with pepper, cover again and cook for a further hour, adding extra stock if necessary.

4 Remove the string, slice the beef thickly, and arrange on a serving dish. Pour over the juices and garnish with spring onions and radish roses.

Monday Curry
John Duhan, Songwriter

After a long frustrating day on the hunt for poetry and melody (the ingredients of song), I like nothing better than to spend an hour or so over the hob humming. I stick to a rota of the same meals each week, starting with this Chinese curry on Monday.

green or yellow peppers
white onions
mushrooms
courgettes
garlic
spring onions, chopped
ginger
2 heaped tsp mild curry powder
pinch chilli powder/chilli flakes
freshly ground black pepper
2-3 tbsp red pesto
olive oil

1 tsp honey
1 tbsp crème fraîche
boiled potatoes, cut in chunks
yellow onions
water chestnuts
bean sprouts
1 tbsp fish sauce
2 tbsp sesame oil
light soy sauce
oyster sauce
brown or white rice for serving

1 Heat the pan and add a splash of boiling water, then add the torn peppers, chopped onions and roughly diced mushrooms. Cover with a lid for a couple of minutes. Add the courgette sticks, chopped garlic, spring onions and ginger. Then sprinkle the curry powder, a pinch of chilli powder or chilli flakes and some ground pepper over the cooking vegetables. Add the red pesto, a splash of olive oil, a spoon of honey and a dollop of crème fraîche and stir. Add chunks of lightly boiled potato and lid.

2 In a separate pan lightly cook rings of onion in a splash of boiling water, add chopped water chestnuts and bean sprouts, lid for a minute or two and drain. Add the fish sauce, sesame oil, a dash of soy sauce and a glug or two of oyster sauce and serve before the vegetables lose their crunch.

3 Serve with boiled brown or white rice.

Strawberry Tiramisu
Eileen Dunne, Broadcaster

Many years ago, a very nice man took me to dinner and I was wearing pink, so I ordered everything pink! Ever since I have thought about replicating the pink menu. Here is the dessert component. This is a French recipe, which tells you to chill the tiramisu for two hours, but I think it needs a lot more.

2 eggs
20g caster sugar
150g mascarpone

450g strawberries
10 meringue shells

1   Separate the eggs, beat the egg yolks with the sugar until pale, and then add in the mascarpone. Beat the egg whites until they form stiff peaks, then incorporate into the mascarpone mixture and whip the lot.

2   Purée half the strawberries and add to this mix to make a strawberry cream. Crush the meringues and chop the rest of the strawberries.

3   In individual bowls, place a layer of strawberry cream, then a layer of meringue and a layer of strawberries. Repeat the layers as necessary and chill before serving.

4   Bon appétit!

CocoChocNut Cookies ('Pam's Pleasures')
Bernard Farrell, Playwright

Pam Nelson lived for many years in the US, then came to Greystones where, for a while, she blessed us with her mouthwatering recipes. She now lives in Sligo but her memory lingers and her reputation remains secure as we often reproduce her delightful dishes and desserts, cakes and cookies, such as these CocoChocNut Cookies, known to us as 'Pam's Pleasures'.

Nobody will be content with just one square, or even two. Easy to make, delicious to eat, never to be forgotten – and here's how all that pleasure can be yours too.

100g butter
250g digestive biscuits,crumbled
200g good quality dark
    chocolate chips

100g desiccated coconut
100g chopped nuts
1 can (400g) condensed milk

1   Preheat the oven to 180°C/gas 4.

2   Melt the butter and pour on to a 33x22cm Swiss roll tin.

3   On the tray, in the following order, shake the biscuit crumb, the chocolate chips, the coconut and the nuts.

4   On top, drizzle the condensed milk and spread over the other ingredients.

5   Bake for about 30 minutes, until golden brown.

6   Remove from the oven and, while still hot, cut into 2-inch squares.

7   Carefully remove from the tin and leave to cool on a rack.

8   When cold, serve up the cookies and enjoy.

Beef Stir Fry
Catherine Fulvio, Chef and Food Writer

You can't get faster than a stir fry. Speed it up even more by asking your butcher to slice the beef for you. You can try this recipe with prawns, pork or chicken too. This recipe is from the 'Speedy Suppers' chapter in my Family Kitchen *cookbook. Enjoy!*

150g medium egg noodles
sunflower oil
250g trimmed lean sirloin, cut
   into slices
2 garlic cloves, sliced
2cm fresh root ginger, grated
1 level tsp Chinese five spice

4 spring onions, finely sliced
1 large pak choi, shredded
   (or spinach)
1 red chilli, finely sliced
1½ tbsp soy sauce (or to taste)
1 tbsp water

1   Cook the noodles according to the instructions on the packet. Drain and set aside.

2   Heat some oil in a wok. Stir fry the beef over a very high heat until golden.

3   Add the garlic, ginger and the Chinese five spice and cook for a further minute.

4   Add the spring onions, pak choi, chilli, soy sauce and water and stir fry until the vegetables are just tender. Add the cooked noodles and toss everything together. Check for seasoning, adding more soy sauce to taste. Divide between four bowls and serve immediately.

Mushroom Soup
Pat Gilroy, Manager, Dublin Senior Football Team

90g butter
2 medium onions, finely chopped
1 clove garlic, crushed
500g mushrooms
2 tbsp plain flour

1 litre hot chicken or
   vegetable stock
1 bay leaf
4 tablespoons cream
Salt and freshly ground black
   pepper to taste

1   Melt the butter in a medium pan and cook the garlic and onions until they are pale golden. This should take 5-6 minutes. Be careful not to burn the garlic.

2   Add the mushrooms and cook over a high heat for 3 minutes, stirring constantly.

3   Stir in the flour and mix well, making sure all the mushrooms are well coated.

4   Pour in the hot chicken stock and bring to the boil. Add the bay leaf and simmer for 10 minutes. Remove the bay leaf and leave the soup to cool for a few minutes.

5   Pour the soup into a food processor or you can use a hand blender. Blend until smooth.

6   Season with salt and pepper. Stir in the cream and it's ready to serve.

Salmon Quiche
Orla Hardiman, Neurologist

While I like cooking, I have a busy job and there isn't much time for cordon bleu, I'm afraid. I can usually rustle up something reasonable within twenty minutes – pan fried pork steak with ginger (fifteen minutes); tortellini carbonara (ten minutes); fish pie (fifteen minutes) or, if I'm home early enough, lasagne (takes forty minutes). This salmon quiche is one of my family's favourites and is usually demolished within fifteen minutes.

Pastry
170g flour
60g butter
pinch salt
cold water

2 boneless salmon fillets
170g cheddar
170g mozzarella
3 eggs
120ml milk
salt and pepper to taste

1   Pre-heat the oven to 190°C/gas 5.

2   Bake the salmon with the garlic in tinfoil for 15-20 minutes.

3   Rub the butter into the flour, to which has been added a pinch of salt, and add enough cold water to make a consistency suitable for rolling.

4   Line a flan dish with the pastry. Place the cooked salmon on the pastry base. Grate the cheddar and cut the mozzarella into small strips. Add to the flan, retaining a sprinkling of cheddar. Beat the eggs and milk, add salt and pepper and pour into the flan dish. Sprinkle the remaining cheddar on top.

5   Bake for approximately 30 minutes.

French Toast with a Twist
Dermot Healy, Writer

2 free range eggs
1 tbsp plain flour
a pinch each turmeric, ground
   coriander and ground
   cinnamon

1 tbsp honey
1 tsp sweet chilli sauce
4 slices good white bread
vegetable oil for frying

1   Beat the eggs and mix in all the other ingredients except the bread. Soak the bread in the mixture for half an hour.

2   Fry each side for 3 minutes.

Roast Beef with Stuffing
Hermitage Green, Folk Rock Band

We are happy to help this great organisation in any way. We remember our dear friend Paul Darbyshire, who was the strength and conditioning coach for the Munster rugby team and in his own unique way became an inspiration and a friend to everyone in the squad.

In June 2011 Paul sadly passed away after battling so courageously with motor neurone disease. He will always be remembered by the Munster supporters and all his friends for everything he brought and the wonderful memories he has left us. We love you and we miss you.
From Barry, Dan, Darragh, Darragh and Dermot.

50g butter
1 medium onion, chopped
50g celery, finely chopped
50g mushrooms, sliced
400g breadcrumbs
½ tsp salt

pinch black pepper
1 tsp dried basil leaves
1 tsp dried parsley flakes
1300g tenderloin roast
4 slices bacon

1 Melt the butter in a skillet and sauté the onion, celery and mushrooms until transparent.

2 Place the breadcrumbs in a large bowl. Mix in the salt, pepper, basil and parsley.

3 Pour in the sautéed vegetables and mix until blended.

4 Make a lengthwise cut ¾ of the way through the tenderloin and place the stuffing mixture lightly in the pocket. Close with toothpicks. Place the slices of bacon diagonally over the pocket.

5 Place meat in an oblong baking dish. Bake, uncovered, at 180°C/gas 4 for an hour (medium rare). This dish will serve eight.

Tom's New York Pasta
Tom Hickey, Actor

tagliatelle or spaghetti for four
   people, cooked according to
   the packet instructions
30g butter
1 tbsp flour
150ml milk
1-2 cloves garlic, crushed

1 tub Philadelphia Light
   cream cheese
lemon juice
1 small packet smoked salmon
   slices
cod's roe or black olives to garnish
black pepper

1 Cook the pasta and drain, reserving a small amount of the cooking water (a tablespoon or so).

2 While the pasta is cooking, gently melt the butter over a low heat; add the flour to cook for one minute, stirring all the time. Gradually add the milk, a few spoonfuls at a time, still stirring, until you have a loose white sauce.

3 Add the garlic and cream cheese and stir until melted. Just before serving, add a few squeezes of lemon juice and the smoked salmon slices.

4 To serve, place tagliatelle ribbons on each dish. Put a portion of the sauce on the centre, with a teaspoon of cod's roe on top to garnish, adding a final squeeze of lemon juice and a twist of black pepper.

Sabina's Treacle and Ginger Bread
President Michael D. Higgins and Sabina Higgins

1 heaped tbsp golden syrup

1 heaped tbsp treacle

110g butter

110g brown sugar

340g flour

1½ tsp bread soda

pinch salt

1 tsp ground ginger

1 tsp cinnamon

3 eggs

1 tsp vanilla essence

120ml milk

1 Melt together the golden syrup, treacle, butter and brown sugar.

2 Sieve together the dry ingredients.

3 Beat together the eggs, vanilla essence and milk and add to the melted mixture.

4 Add all the dry ingredients and mix well.

5 Pour into lined tins and bake at 190-200°C/gas mark 5-6 for approximately an hour.

Chicken and Broccoli Bake
Amy Huberman, Actor and Author

I got this recipe from a friend who was sick of hearing me harping on about really needing to learn to cook one of these fine days. She promised me this recipe was a total cinch, which it is. I think this was the first proper dinner I ever cooked, although I did nearly kill a few people my first go by confusing curry powder with chilli powder. I always come back to this dish if I want to cook something quick and wholesome and deliciously tasty. Enjoy!

olive oil for frying
1 large onion, finely chopped
4 chicken breasts cut
    into small chunks
250g button mushrooms, halved
450g broccoli, broken into florets

2 tins cream of chicken soup
2 tsps medium curry powder
50g breadcrumbs
50g grated hard cheese
    such as cheddar
salt and pepper

1   Preheat the oven to 220°C/gas 7.

2   Sweat the onion on low heat for 1 minute to soften but not 'fry' it. Increase the heat and seal the chicken pieces but do not cook through.

3   Toss in the mushrooms and mix with the chicken and onions. Remove from the heat.

4   Boil the broccoli for 3 minutes.

5   Mix the soup and the curry powder and season with salt and pepper.

6   Put the chicken, onions, mushrooms and broccoli in an ovenproof dish or casserole dish. Pour over the soup mixture, top with breadcrumbs and sprinkle with the grated cheese.

7   Bake for approximately 30 minutes.

T-Bone Steak and Sides
Tom Jordan, Actor

Starter
Italian antipasto from any good supermarket
cantaloupe melon

Main
large portobello mushroom
2 tbsp duck or liver paté
2 medium potatoes per person, peeled and cut into chunks
handful of chopped onion
small York cabbage
knob of butter
1 T-Bone steak per person

Dessert
250g punnet strawberries
carton best quality shop-bought ice cream
small carton cream

1   Arrange the antipasto on a tray or platter with wedges of cantaloupe melon.

2   Remove the stalk from the portobello mushroom and hollow out the centre. Fill with duck or liver paté and bake in the middle of the oven at 180°C/gas 4 for 15 minutes.

3   Boil the potatoes and mash with as much butter or cream as you think fit, adding the raw chopped onion at the end. Season with salt and freshly ground pepper. Finely slice the York cabbage and braise in a saucepan with a knob of butter for just a few minutes to keep it crunchy.

4   Grill or fry the T-bone steak. If the meat is good you can cook it without any seasoning. Serve with the mash, cabbage and stuffed mushroom.

5   For dessert, serve the strawberries with the ice cream and freshly whipped cream.

Stir Fried Pork Fillet
Enda Kenny, An Taoiseach

I like this particular dish because it is very quick, very simple,
full of flavour and reasonably healthy.

olive oil for frying
1 red pepper, finely chopped
1 stalk celery, finely chopped
1 carrot, finely sliced
2 shallots, finely chopped
2 cloves garlic, finely chopped
1cm piece root ginger, grated

1 pork fillet, thinly sliced
Chinese five spice
soy sauce to taste
1 tbsp honey
250g sliced button mushrooms
salt and freshly ground black
   pepper to season

1 Gently fry the pepper, celery, carrot and shallots in a little oil in a frying pan or wok.

2 Add the garlic and ginger.

3 Add thin slices of the pork. Stir well, increase heat, season and add five spice powder to taste.

4 Cook for 3-4 minutes.

5 Add soy sauce, honey and mushrooms, reduce heat and cook for a further 3-4 minutes.

6 Adjust seasoning.

7 Serve with egg noodles and prawn crackers.

Piccata Milanese with Dressed Rocket Leaves

Bobby Kerr, Businessman

8 medallions pork fillet

5 egg yolks

50g finely grated Parmesan

50ml fresh cream

2 tsp fresh parsley, finely chopped

2 tbsp plain flour, seasoned with
    salt and freshly ground black
    pepper

Rocket Salad

250g washed rocket

half small red onion, thinly sliced

1 clove garlic, crushed

50g toasted pine nuts

couple of cherry tomatoes (for
    colour and taste)

2 tbsp honey

4 tbsp balsamic vinegar

4 tbsp olive oil

1   Flatten the pork fillets with a rolling pin between two sheets of clingfilm. Mix the egg yolks, Parmesan, cream and parsley together in a bowl.

2   Place the dry ingredients for the salad in a salad bowl. Prepare the dressing by mixing oil, vinegar and honey is a small bowl or jar. Dress the salad, toss and set aside.

3   Dip the pork fillets first in the seasoned flour, then in the egg mix, making sure each medallion is well coated. Pan fry the medallions in olive oil for about 3 to 4 minutes each side until they are golden brown.

4   Divide the salad between four warm plates and place two pork medallions on top of each. Finish with a few shavings of Parmesan and a few drops of balsamic vinegar.

Strawberry and Mascarpone Tart

Laura Kilkenny, The Wooden Spoon,
Killaloe, County Clare

This recipe was kindly donated in memory of Carmel Harrington, late of St Munchin's College, Limerick, who passed away due to motor neurone disease. Carmel worked at the college for more than thirty years but it was not merely a place of employment to her. She gave to the fabric of the college, looking after and steering generations of students, who recall her quiet guidance and support with affection and warmth. This is a really lovely summertime treat, especially scrumptious when strawberries are in season.

Base
400g digestive biscuits, crushed
250g butter, melted

Topping
2 large eggs
2 tbsp caster sugar
500g mascarpone
1 lemon, zest and juice
500g strawberries or another
    fruit of your choice

1   Grease and line a 20cm loose-bottomed tart tin with clingfilm or baking parchment. In a bowl, combine the melted butter with the crushed biscuits. Place this mixture into the prepared tin and compress. Place in the fridge to harden.

2   Separate the eggs. In one bowl, place the sugar and the yolks and whisk until pale and fluffy. Then add the mascarpone and lemon juice and zest and whisk together.

3   In another very clean bowl, whisk the egg whites until they are stiff. Fold the whites into the cheese mixture and pour on to the prepared base. Slice the strawberries and arrange nicely on top. If you have any cheeky chocolate in the house melt a little and drizzle over the top for extra yumminess.

4   Chill before serving.

Traditional Colcannon, Tipperary Style
John Lonergan, Former Governor, Mountjoy Prison

When I was growing up in Tipperary in the 1950s one of the things I most looked forward to every year was the colcannon my mother made, or should I say cooked, when the new potatoes were ready for eating. This was normally around mid-June and I can still remember the thrill of digging out the new potatoes – or spuds as we called them in those days. My father closely supervised this annual event and personally selected the stalks that were ready for digging. As each stalk was dug up clusters of beautiful snow-white potatoes fell from the dark brown clay and looked like big pearls on the ground. Ah, definitely, no spuds like them nowadays!

The spuds were put in a galvanised bucket and brought to the kitchen. There my mother washed them in cold water and boiled them in a big black metal pot over the open fire. When they were cooked she mashed them in their skins, adding hot milk and a fistful of home-grown scallions. At dinnertime she used a wooden spoon to put the colcannon out on the plates. Then just before eating we always put a lump of butter in a hollow in the centre and as the butter melted it dribbled across the colcannon. It was gorgeous. Now I know that some people will say that what I have outlined is champ, not colcannon, but we called it colcannon and that's good enough for me.

10 medium-large peeled potatoes
small bunch of fresh scallions
or half head of cabbage

250ml hot milk
Salt and pepper
120g butter

1   Boil or steam potatoes until cooked and chop scallions or cabbage finely. In the case of the cabbage cook in a little water until tender, in the case of the scallions boil gently in the milk until soft.

2   Drain the cabbage and mix with potatoes or pour the hot milk and scallions on to the potatoes and mash into a smooth mixture. Add salt, pepper and butter. Serve on hot plates.

Tom Yum Soup

Jack Lukeman, Singer

*Thailand is one of the most beautiful countries to visit and its food is my
favourite. This soup is both healthy and tasty.*

1 litre water
4-10 crushed hot red chillies
2 stalks lemongrass
   (sliced into 3cm long pieces)
70g sliced galangal
1 tbsp shrimp paste
70g sliced onion
70g sliced tomatoes
10 shrimps/prawns or chopped
   chicken breast pieces

125g sliced mushrooms
4 tbsp fish sauce
½ tsp salt
1 tsp sugar
4 tsp lime juice
2 tbsp chopped spring onions
2 stems fresh coriander
4 stems fresh parsley
6 kaffir lime leaves

1 Put the water in a pot and heat until boiling. Add the chillies, lemongrass, galangal,
   shrimp paste and onion and cook until fragrant.

2 Add the tomatoes, shrimp (prawns or chicken) and mushrooms and cook through gently,
   then add the fish sauce, salt and sugar. Stir thoroughly.

3 Add the lime juice, spring onion, coriander, parsley and lime leaves. Stir thoroughly and
   serve immediately.

Iveragh Harvest Chowder

Kathleen Lynch TD, Minister of State for Disability,
Equality and Mental Health

900g mixed fish, such as ling,
   cod, haddock or trout,
   chopped roughly
2 onions chopped
6 sticks of celery, diced
8 carrots, sliced
½ chilli, finely chopped
1 red pepper chopped
4 potatoes, diced
2 cloves garlic, crushed
black pepper and salt to season

4 tomatoes, diced
1 head of broccoli, separated
   into florets
I packet of broccoli/cauliflower
   soup to thicken
100g freshly cooked
   peeled shrimps
20 cooked cockles removed
   from shell
300ml fresh cream

1   Cook the fish for 15 minutes in seasoned water, them remove from stock and allow to cool. Remove skin and any bones from the fish. Use the stock as a base for the chowder.

2   Add water to the fish stock to half-fill a large family pot. Add onions, celery, carrots, chilli, red pepper, potatoes, garlic and seasoning and allow to cook for 15 minutes. Add tomatoes, broccoli and packet soup and simmer for a further 10 minutes. Add the fish, shrimp and cockles and simmer gently for 10 minutes. Check the seasoning.

3   Add 300ml lightly whipped cream.

4   Serve with a large bowl of flowery boiled jacket potatoes.

Wedding Cake
John MacKenna, Writer

This is a recipe from Richmond's Cookery Recipes, *published in 1903. The book belonged to Brigid Keogh of Michael Street in Kilkenny. Not only is the cake delicious but making it will get you fit! This is the wedding cake recipe word for word from the book (with ingredients converted to metric).*

1.4kg flour	30g mixed spices
1.4kg butter	½ grated nutmeg
1.1kg mixed peel	½ pint sherry
454g sweet almonds	rind of 3 lemons
16 eggs	salt
680g caster sugar	

1   Beat the butter to a cream; add the sugar, eggs and flour. Mix well; add all the other ingredients, the currants being cleaned, the peel cut into small pieces and the almonds blanched and finely chopped. Beat all together for one hour.

2   Line a large baking tin with double paper, well-greased. Pour in the mixture, which should not fill the tin, and bake in a moderate oven for five to six hours.

3   This cake can be halved by using half the ingredients and beating for half an hour.

Irish Stew

Jimmy Magee, Broadcaster

My son, Paul, passed away from MND in May 2009. I hope for all the families, friends and the extended MND community that we find that elusive cure and achieve the vision of the IMNDA: together we will beat motor neurone disease. This is one of my favourite main courses for lunch or dinner, especially in the winter.

1kg neck or shoulder of lamb or 2 gigot chops per person
bouquet garni (sprig parsley, sprig thyme and 2 bay leaves tied with twine)
2 medium onions, finely chopped
salt and freshly ground black pepper

2 medium carrots, chopped into bite-sized pieces
1 leek, chopped into bite-sized pieces (optional)
1 small turnip, chopped into bite-sized pieces (optional)
3 large or 6 small potatoes, peeled and cut into large chunks
finely chopped parsley to garnish

1   Remove the meat from the bone, trim off and discard all the fat and cut into cubes. Your butcher may be happy to do this for you but be sure to keep the bones as they will intensify the flavour of the stew.

2   Put the meat, bones, bouquet garni, onions, seasoning, carrots and other vegetables (if used) into a large pot and cover with water. Simmer gently for an hour.

3   Skim off any foam that has risen to the top of the cooking liquid. Add the potatoes and simmer for a further 25 minutes. Check that the meat and vegetables are tender.

4   Remove the bones and the bouquet garni. Check the seasoning. Garnish with chopped parsley and serve with buttery mashed potatoes or, as the dish already contains potatoes, hunks of soda bread.

Hake with Cassoulet of Beans and Chorizo
Neven Maguire, Chef and Food Writer

Hake has a lovely soft texture and slight sweetness when it's very fresh. The combination of the chorizo and beans gives this dish a real Spanish flavour. It can be cooked up to two days in advance and kept covered in the fridge.

2 tbsp rapeseed oil
100g raw chorizo
60g mixed dried beans
   (such as haricot, cannellini,
   borlotti or black-eyed beans)
150ml vegetable stock
1 tbsp softened butter
1 tsp sea salt

1 tsp freshly ground black pepper
2 tsp chopped flat-leaf parsley
1 tsp snipped fresh chives
4 x 150g (5oz) skinless hake fillets,
   pin bones removed
garnish: red pepper gel, basil
   purée, red pepper foam,
   fresh micro basil

1 Preheat the oven to 200°C/gas mark 6. Heat 1 tablespoon of the rapeseed oil in a heavy-based pan over a medium heat. Add the chorizo and sauté for 2-3 minutes, until sizzling. Remove the chorizo and drain on kitchen paper.

2 Place the beans in a large pan with plenty of water and a good pinch of salt. Bring to a simmer and cook for 20-30 minutes, until tender. Drain and refresh under cold running water.

3 Place the stock, the butter, the reserved cooked chorizo and the beans in a pan and bring to the boil, then reduce the heat and simmer for a few minutes, until warmed through. Season to taste and stir in the parsley and chives. Keep warm.

4 Arrange the hake on a piece of parchment paper in a steamer. Drizzle with the remaining tablespoon of oil and steam for 8-10 minutes, until just cooked and tender. The cooking time obviously depends on the thickness of the fish fillets.

5 To serve, spoon the bean and chorizo cassoulet on to the centre of each warmed plate and arrange the hake on top, skin side up. Garnish with the red pepper gel and basil purée, then spoon over the pepper foam and scatter with the micro basil.

Green Beef Curry with Thai Aubergine
Leo Moran, Guitarist, the Saw Doctors

*This is a recipe I've often helped Eleanor, my partner, put together, not just
for gatherings in the house but for the many bands and their crews who have
graced Campbell's Tavern in Cloughanover, near Headford in County Galway,
where she works, with their talent and hard work.
The pot has always been licked spotless!*

1 tbsp vegetable oil
45ml green curry paste
600ml coconut milk
450g sirloin of beef
4 kaffir lime leaves, torn
1-2 tbsp Thai fish sauce

1 tsp soft light brown sugar
150g small Thai aubergines or
    baby aubergines, halved
2 fresh green chillies and a small
    handful of Thai basil, to garnish

1   Heat the oil in a wok or large pan. Add the green curry paste and fry gently until the paste begins to release its fragrant aromas. Pour in half the coconut milk, a little at a time.

2   Cook over a medium heat for 5-6 minutes, until the oil begins to separate and an oily sheen appears on the surface.

3   Cut the beef into long, thin slices and add to the pan with the kaffir lime leaves, fish sauce, sugar and aubergines.

4   Bring back to a simmer and cook gently until the meat and aubergines are tender.

5   Finely shred the green chillies and use to garnish the curry along with the Thai basil leaves.

6   Serve with plain boiled rice or noodles.

Ann's Fish Dish
Eamon Morrissey, Actor

*I am forwarding my wife Ann's fish dish. It is simple and easy.
I know, I have cooked it myself. A glass of decent white wine
to drink while it is in the oven is a help.*

2 large fillets fresh cod or haddock
with skin removed
1 tbsp Dijon mustard

120g gruyère, grated
1 small carton (125ml) fresh cream
salt and black pepper to season

1   Cut the fish into four pieces and place in a baking dish. Mix the mustard with the cream and pour over the fish. Sprinkle with grated gruyère and add salt and pepper to taste.

2   Bake at 180°C/gas 4 for approximately 20 minutes. Serve with creamed potatoes and baby spinach or asparagus.

Banana Bread
Caroline Murphy and Sean O'Rourke, Broadcasters

Three of Sean and Caroline's four sons are very keen on bananas, so in their house they disappear quickly. But it's hard to keep track of who is around, and sometimes they both buy them in bulk so the fruit bowl does occasionally groan with a few ripening leftovers. That's when they call on their daughter, Aisling, for one of Caroline's favourites, banana bread.

225g plain flour,
1 tsp salt
1 heaped tsp baking powder
1 tsp cinnamon
110g caster sugar
1 egg, beaten

75ml sunflower oil
1 tsp pure vanilla essence
4 medium ripe bananas, mashed
65g pecans, chopped, or 100g
   chocolate chips (optional)

1   Pre-heat the oven to 180°C/gas 4. Line the base of a 1kg loaf tin with baking parchment and brush some sunflower oil around the sides.

2   Sift the flour, salt, baking powder and cinnamon into a bowl.

3   Stir in the caster sugar.

4   Combine the egg, oil and vanilla essence and add to the dry ingredients, mixing well.

5   With a fork, fold in the banana (and nuts or chocolate) but don't overbeat.

6   Transfer to the prepared loaf tin and bake in the oven for 50-60 minutes until the top is golden brown and the loaf is springy to touch.

7   Leave the bread in the tin for 5 minutes, then turn out onto a wire cooking rack. It will need an hour to cool.

8   This freezes well and if sliced before frozen, can be popped directly into the toaster.

Gigot Chop Stew
David Norris, Senator

*The reason I chose this is because it was a favourite recipe of my late aunt.
I always used to love the smell of the stew bubbling away on the stove in
her house in Ballsbridge. It made the place feel so homely and comforting.*

3 to 4 gigot chops
2 to 3 medium potatoes
2 large carrots
2 large parsnips
2 sticks celery
2 large onions

2 stock cubes
2 sprigs rosemary
good pinch ground cumin
sprig thyme
salt and pepper

1   First of all I get three to four good gigot chops and I hack them up into small pieces but I do leave the bones in as I think they give a flavour.

2   I sprinkle a few of the pieces into a large saucepan followed by chopped vegetables, potato, onion, carrot, celery, parsnip. I put another layer of meat, another layer of vegetables etc.

3   On top of this I crumble the stock cubes, fill the pot up with water and add the rosemary, cumin and thyme.

4   Then over a period of days I boil the bejasus out of it. What I do is I let it get to the boil then when it's started to boil furiously I turn it right down and let it simmer.

5   I do this a few hours every day. It can of course be eaten after about two or three hours on the first day but it's much better left and re-boiled whenever you think of it over the next day or two.

6   You will eventually end up with the most wonderful mushy stew with delicious tender meat. Do be careful of the bones.

Pulled Pork

Paul O'Connell, Rugby Player

shoulder of pork, deboned
   by your butcher if possible
100g brown sugar
50g paprika
1 tbsp black pepper
1 tbsp salt
1 tbsp chilli powder

1 tbsp garlic powder
1 tbsp onion powder
1 tsp cayenne pepper
1 tbsp ground cumin
1 litre of Coca-Cola
   (not sugar free)

1   Mix together all the dry ingredients and rub well into the shoulder of pork. Put the meat into a large plastic bag with any remaining spice mix and leave in the fridge for up to 48 hours.

2   Set the oven to 150ºC/gas 2 and cook the pork for up to 12 hours in Coca-Cola. Baste occasionally and add more liquid if it looks like drying out.

3   Shred the meat and serve on fresh baps with lots of crispy salad and coleslaw.

Olive Bread
Mary O'Donnell, Writer

This bread is delicious with any medium-bodied red wine.

250g plain flour
4 eggs
1 wine glass olive oil
1 wine glass white wine
dash of vermouth
150g grated cheddar

150g pitted green olives, plain or stuffed with pimientos
200g chopped smoked streaky bacon
salt and freshly ground black pepper

1 Grease 2 x 500g loaf tins. Mix all the ingredients together in a bowl and divide the mixture between the two tins.

2 Bake for about an hour at 180ºC/gas 6.

Éclairs
Mary O'Rourke, Politician

The Hodson Bay Hotel was my home when I was younger. I attended boarding school up to the age of seventeen and when I came home from the holidays, meals were on tap so I never bothered to find out about cooking. When I went away to college, to UCD, I got all my meals in Loreto Hall. Things changed when I met Enda, fell in love and married. I literally couldn't boil an egg!

My sister-in-law, Ann Devine, offered herself as a cookery instructor. I can vividly remember her coming to visit me one Saturday. Ann was a great teacher and I mastered the difficult art of perfect chocolate éclairs. They became a household favourite and I gained quite a reputation as a cook thanks to Ann's éclairs. The friendship forged that Saturday is still as strong as ever.

140ml water   3 eggs
140g butter   50g dark chocolate
140g plain flour   whipped cream

1   Bring the water and 110g of the butter to a boil in a saucepan. Stir in the sifted flour all at once. Cook the batter over a low heat, stirring until it is smooth and elastic and comes away cleanly from the sides of the pan.

2   Cool the mixture, stirring occasionally.

3   Beat in the eggs, one by one, taking care to blend one egg fully before adding another.

4   Pipe the mixture on to a greased baking tin in three-inch fingers and bake for 20-25 minutes in a moderate oven (190°C/gas 5).

5   When cool, slit the side of each éclair and fill with whipped cream.

6   Gently melt the remaining butter and chocolate in a bowl over a saucepan of simmering water, making sure the bowl does not touch the water. Spoon the chocolate sauce on top of the éclairs. Leave to set before eating.

Fillet of Cod with Clonakilty Blackpudding

Sonia O'Sullivan, Athlete

*I fly back and forth to and from Ireland so much that I often find myself
shopping for food at Wrights of Howth in Dublin Airport and always
picking up Clonakilty Blackpudding. This recipe is one I created myself;
it is very simple but one of the tastiest combinations I know.*

4 large fillets of cod
250g Clonakilty Blackpudding

100g mushrooms, chopped
200g cherry tomatoes

1 Pre-heat the oven to 180°C/gas 4.

2 Place the fish in a large casserole dish, crumble black pudding on top and surround the
fish with chopped mushrooms and cherry tomatoes.

3 Pour a dash of olive oil around the edges to prevent the food from sticking to the dish.

4 Bake for 20-30 minutes.

5 Serve with broccoli or asparagus and small potatoes roasted in olive oil with rosemary.

Ped Grob Gap Plum Dong
(Crispy Roast Duck with Pickled Plums)

Brent Pope, Rugby Commentator

I have loved Thai food since my days of travelling and sampling food cooked by locals on a simple wok, more or less on the side of the road. I also love duck, although it is hard to get perfect. The important thing is to cook the duck just long enough: it should be crispy yet pink inside. The plums sound complicated but are easy to prepare. Make them as hot as you like.

4 boneless duck breasts
3 spring onions, finely chopped
2 cloves garlic, crushed
4 tbsp oyster sauce
1 tbsp vegetable oil

Pickled plums
55g caster sugar
4 tbsp white wine vinegar
1 chilli, deseeded and
    finely chopped
½ tsp salt
4 red plums, stoned and quartered

1   Make diagonal cuts into the skin of the duck. Combine the spring onion, garlic and oyster sauce and spread over the duck. Cover the marinated meat and place in the fridge for an hour.

2   Meanwhile, to make the plum sauce, put all the remaining ingredients, except the plums, into a saucepan and simmer for ten minutes. Add the plums and simmer for a further five minutes until they soften. Remove from the heat and leave to cool.

3   Preheat the oven to 200°C/gas 6. In a frying pan sear the duck breasts, skin side down, for two to three minutes until browned. Turn over and sear for a further two minutes.

4   Transfer the duck to a roasting tin, cover with tinfoil, and cook for about twelve minutes.

5   Remove the foil and let the meat stand for ten minutes. Cut the duck diagonally into slices and serve with plum sauce on a bed of noodles or rice with a side dish of stir fried vegetables.

Somewhat Samosas

Suzanne Power, Writer

This recipe came out of a leftover curry. We're not scientific chefs so apologies if the measurements are a bit askew. The people of India may find the use of filo pastry heinous, but it really does work!

2 diced carrots
130g lentils
130g diced potato
70g frozen peas
1 onion, chopped
vegetable oil for frying

curry paste to taste
1 tsp cumin seeds
1 packet filo pastry
vegetable oil for brushing
½ tin (about 200g) tomatoes

1   Preheat the oven to 200°C/gas 6.

2   Put diced carrots in water to par-boil. Add lentils to the water when the carrots are slightly soft. Add the potatoes to cook after 5 minutes but make sure they don't overcook – you want the potatoes to hold their shape and the lentils to be firm to the touch. Finally, after another 5 minutes, add the frozen peas.

3   Fry the chopped onion in oil and add curry paste and cumin seeds. Add the half tin of tomatoes and boiled vegetables, mix and hope!

4   Open the filo pastry. Have a little vegetable oil ready with a pastry brush. Cut pastry into quarter squares. Take 2-3 sheets of cut pastry and spoon the mixture in. Fold it as you would an old fashioned nappy on a baby but leave out the pin as it doesn't taste good! Paint on a little vegetable oil.

5   Put the samosas on a tray in the oven and bake for 10-15 minutes, until golden and crispy.

Pork Steak à la Mo
Martina Stanley, Actor

*This is a recipe I got many moons ago from the late, great Maureen Toal.
I've cooked it many many times and always think of her when I do.
Thanks Mo! Easy peasy!*

1 large pork steak
2 cloves garlic, finely chopped
I tbsp soy sauce

olive oil and butter for frying
1 small carton (125ml) cream

1   Cut the pork steak into thin slices, place in a flat dish and sprinkle with garlic. Splash with the soy sauce and cover the dish with clingfilm. Leave to marinate in the fridge for an hour.

2   Pan-fry the pork slices in batches in a little olive oil and butter.

3   To make the sauce, empty any left-over marinade into the pan and add the cream. Bring to the boil and simmer for a few minutes to combine the flavours. Put the cooked meat back into the sauce, sprinkle with chopped coriander and serve with sauté potatoes or rice.

Boeuf Bourguignon
Pat Shortt, Actor

150g bacon
1 tbsp olive oil
1300g lean stewing beef, diced.
1 carrot, diced
1 onion, sliced
1 tsp salt and ¼ tsp pepper
2 tbsp flour
500ml Chianti

500ml brown beef stock
1 tbsp tomato purée
2 cloves garlic, crushed
½ tsp dried thyme
1 bay leaf
450g mushrooms and 1 onion,
    chopped and sautéed in butter
parsley sprigs for garnishing

1   Preheat oven to 220°C/gas 7. In a casserole, sauté the bacon in the oil over moderate heat for 2-3 minutes to brown. Remove to a side dish. Reheat until fat is almost smoking. Dry the beef with paper towels; it will not brown if it is damp. Sauté it, a few pieces at a time, in the hot oil and bacon fat until nicely browned on all sides. Add it to the bacon. In the same fat, brown the sliced vegetables. Pour out the sautéing fat. Return the beef and bacon to the casserole and toss with salt and pepper. Then sprinkle on the flour and toss again to coat the beef lightly. Set casserole uncovered in the middle of the pre-heated oven for 4 minutes. Toss the meat and return to oven for a further 4 minutes. (This browns the flour and covers the meat with a light crust.) Remove the casserole and turn the oven down to 160°C/gas 3. Stir in the wine and enough stock barely to cover the meat. Add the tomato purée, garlic and herbs. Bring to a simmer on top of the stove, then cover the casserole and set in the lower third of the oven. Regulate heat so liquid simmers very slowly for 2½-3 hours. The meat is done when a fork pierces it easily.

2   While the beef is cooking, prepare the mushrooms and onions and set aside. When the meat is tender, pour the contents of the casserole into a sieve set over a saucepan. Wash out the casserole and return the beef and bacon to it. Distribute the cooked onions and mushrooms over the meat. Skim the fat off the sauce and simmer for a minute or two, skimming off additional fat as it rises. Check carefully for seasoning. Pour the sauce over the meat and vegetables, cover the casserole and simmer for 2 to 3 minutes, basting the meat and vegetables with the sauce several times. Serve in its casserole, or arrange the stew on a platter surrounded by potatoes, noodles or rice and garnished with parsley.

Chicken Curry
Pierce Turner, Singer

Curry sauce
2½ tbsp butter
2 large onions, chopped
1 large apple, chopped,
 including skin and seeds
2½ tbsp flour
1 cup milk
2 organic chicken stock cubes
1½ tsp curry powder (or to taste)

The 'big pot'
2 tbsp grapeseed oil
6 cloves garlic, finely chopped

small piece of root ginger,
 finely chopped
about a dozen mushrooms,
 chopped
750g chicken breast fillets,
 preferably organic or free
 range, cut into chunky pieces
2 large carrots
juice of 1 lemon
salt for seasoning
soy sauce (optional)
¾ tsp Marmite
1 tsp mango chutney

1 For the curry sauce, melt the butter in a saucepan. Sauté one chopped onion and the apple until well softened, stirring regularly. Add the flour and stir frantically. Quickly add the milk and the chicken stock cubes, already dissolved in a cup of boiling water, and keep whisking until the sauce thickens. Turn down the heat and add 1½ teaspoons curry powder, or to taste. I like it medium hot. Turn off the heat and let the sauce sit.

2 For the 'big pot', put a saucepan on a medium to high heat and add 2 tbsp grapeseed oil. Sauté the finely chopped garlic and ginger. Add the chopped onion and mushrooms. Stir in the chicken pieces and the chopped carrots. Add the lemon juice, salt to taste or soy sauce, then the Marmite. Put the lid on the pot and allow the meat and vegetables to cook for 45 minutes on a low to medium heat, stirring occasionally.

3 When the contents of the big pot are cooked, stir in the curry sauce. Add 1 teaspoon mango chutney and allow to simmer for 30 minutes. This curry improves if you allow it to stand and reheat it later.

4 Serve with organic brown basmati rice, cooked according to the packet instructions.

Clonakilty Whitepudding and Mushroom Frittata

Colette Twomey, CEO and Co-Founder, Clonakilty Blackpudding

280g Clonakilty Whitepudding, roughly chopped
rapeseed oil
50g butter

400g mixed mushrooms (such as button, Paris browns), chopped
8 large free range eggs
50ml cream
salt and pepper

1   Preheat oven to 180°C/gas 4. On a medium heat place the Clonakilty Whitepudding on a 20cm non-stick frying pan with a deep base. Cook to colour and warm through, remove and set aside for later.

2   Increase the heat on the pan and coat with rapeseed oil. Add the butter and the chopped mushrooms and cook until golden brown.

3   Remove the mushrooms from the pan and set aside with the Clonakilty Whitepudding.

4   In a large bowl whisk the eggs with the cream and season with salt and pepper.

5   Mix the cooked Clonakilty White pudding and mushrooms into the egg mixture to coat. This will ensure that the ingredients are evenly dispersed through your frittata.

6   Place the frittata mixture into the same pan and with a spatula move the mixture away from the bottom until it starts to set.

7   Transfer to the pre-heated oven for 10-15 minutes to cook through.

8   Run a spatula around the sides to ensure that your frittata will turn out. Slice into portions and serve with a mixed green salad for a perfect lunch or brunch!

Lamb Chops and Mash
Ruby Walsh, Jockey and Trainer

Yours is a wonderful cause – an illness that really is a life sentence – and I am sorry as cooking is my Achilles heel as regards anything that needs a recipe! Lamb chops and mash is about it!

2 quality lamb loin chops per person
2 tbsp oil
3-4 tbsp seeded mustard
2 tbsp chopped fresh herbs (parsley, chives, thyme)
salt and pepper to taste

4-5 large potatoes, peeled and chopped
butter and milk for mash
3 large carrots, peeled and thickly sliced
drizzle of olive oil
chopped chives (optional)

1   Rub the lamb with oil, mustard and herbs and season with salt and pepper.

2   Brown the chops on both sides over a moderate heat, then transfer to a pre-heated oven, 180°C/gas 4, and cook to your liking. Or you can pan fry or grill or BBQ them 2-3 minutes per side if you like them rare.

3   Cook the potatoes in boiling salted water until tender. Drain, then add a knob of butter and a little milk and mash. Season to taste.

4   Simmer the carrots in boiling water until tender. Drain and add the oil, season with salt and pepper and sprinkle over the chives.

Really Good Southern Fried Chicken

Grace Wells, Writer

This really is delicious.

4-6 chicken breasts cut into medium chunks or strips
250g natural yogurt
2 tbsp chopped garlic (about 6 cloves)
½ tsp ground cayenne pepper
1 tsp ground cumin
½ tsp mace (optional)
1 tsp ground nutmeg
1 tsp paprika
1 tsp ground ginger
2 tsp freshly ground black pepper
1 tsp dried basil
2 tsp dried sage
2 tsp dried thyme
1 tsp salt
250g plain flour

1 Put the chicken pieces in a large glass or stainless steel bowl. Stir the garlic into the yogurt. Pour it over the chicken and turn until the meat is coated and submerged.

2 Marinate in the fridge for at least 30 minutes to an hour.

3 Meanwhile, combine the spices, herbs and salt in a bowl. Put the flour in a large clear freezer bag and sprinkle the herb and spice mixture into it. Close the bag and shake well until the seasoning is evenly distributed.

4 Heat about half an inch of oil in a frying pan until hot but not smoking.

5 Lift the chicken pieces out of the yogurt marinade one at a time and drop into the bag with the seasoned flour. Close the bag and shake until the chicken is well coated. Assemble a few ready-coated pieces on a plate. This is a bit messy, so have some kitchen paper on standby.

6 Fry the chicken pieces, turning once, and cooking for about three minutes on each side. Drain on kitchen paper before serving.

Index of Recipes

Index

filo pastry 110
fish sauce 53, 82, 92
French fried onions 12

galangal 82
ganache 29
garam masala 18, 32
garlic 15, 18, 19, 20, 22, 25, 31, 32, 35, 37, 41,
    47, 49, 50, 53, 59, 61, 62, 68, 75, 77, 84, 101,
    109, 112, 115, 117, 123
gherkins 22
ginger 18, 19, 25, 53, 59, 62, 70, 75, 117, 123
ground ginger 25, 70, 123
glacé cherries 38
golden syrup 70
gram flour 22
grapeseed oil 29, 117
green curry paste 92
gruyère 93
Guinness 15

haddock 84, 93
hake 91
haricot beans 91
hazelnuts 29
honey 20, 25, 53, 65, 75, 77
horseradish 12

kaffir lime leaves 82, 92

lamb
gigot chops 88, 98
    loin chops 120
    rack 20
    shoulder 88
leek 88
lemon 22, 25, 68, 79, 117
lemongrass 82
lentils 18, 19, 110
lime juice 82
lime leaves 82, 92
ling 84
linguine 31
lovage 49

mace 123
mackerel 16
mango chutney 117
Marmite 117
mascarpone 54, 79
mayonnaise 13, 22
meatballs 35
meringue 54
mint 20
mixed peel 87
mixed spices 87
mozzarella 62
mushrooms 18, 37, 53, 61, 67, 82, 107, 115, 117
    porcini 37
    portobello 72
    button 16, 71, 75
mustard 12

nutmeg 42, 87, 123

oats, rolled 27
olive oil 12, 13, 15, 18, 20, 25, 35, 37, 41, 47,
    49, 53, 71, 75, 77, 103, 107, 112, 115, 120
olives 68, 103
onions, red 18, 41, 77
onions 11, 12, 15, 18, 19, 25, 26, 31, 35, 49, 50,
    53, 59, 61, 71, 72, 84, 88, 98, 109, 115, 117
oyster sauce 53, 109

pak choi, 59
paprika 18
Parmesan 11, 16, 35, 37, 41, 42, 43, 77
parsley 12, 13, 15, 20, 22, 26, 35, 37, 67, 77, 82,
    88, 91, 115, 120
parsnip 98
peas 37, 41, 53, 110
pecans 97
linguine 31
peperoncino 47
pepper, red 11, 12, 13, 15, 16, 18, 19, 20, 22,
    25, 26, 31, 32, 35, 42, 47, 49, 50, 53, 61, 62,
    67, 68, 71, 75, 77, 81, 84, 88, 91, 93, 98, 101,
    103, 115, 118, 120, 123
pepper, yellow 53